Sharon R

# GOOD FRIDAY

Toby's KS1 & KS2 Stuff
Part I Poems & Short Stories
By Sharon Rose

Illustrator Richard Uff

Editor Kamala Ram

# Good Friday

© 2021  Rose Fortitude

ISBN:  9798725626551

i

# Good Friday

Good Friday

## DEDICATION

In the service of our God, a Servant King.
For the inspiration of His Children
everywhere.  Jesus loves you.

Sharon Rose

# CONTENTS

Good Friday

# ACKNOWLEDGEMENT

Thanking God for the inspiration of his Word. A lot of people have also inspired this work. Thanking Toby for helping me to view Easter through 7/8 year old lenses and his magnificent ever delightful characters. Including Mr Bean and Usain Bolt and the parent(s) who bought the original amateur version. To my illustrious Illustrator, Richard Uff. For vividly bringing the stories alive!

Ugandan readers who believed in the content so much so that it was sold out at launch – thank you! Keep your bright minds forever nurtured. Early purchasers of the original edition are entitled to a discount upon producing an original copy. To the accommodating and kind Association of Ugandan Writers (cannot now remember their address) who provided professional support and were available to guide me. To all those believing in my ability to see this project through, helping along the way by either recommending Publishing houses, Artists, Editors, Amazon's KDP, website developers, countless Youtube self publishing gurus, marketing tools and proofreading volunteers. Thank you ever so much. This is the outcome of our collective contribution. Be blessed. You are a blessing.

# Good Friday

Sharon Rose

# DISCLAIMER

All errors are mine. There is room for improvement and all honest feedback would be welcome.

Sharon Rose

Sharon Rose

## LIGHTNING DOG

Dogs chase
Cats run
Cheetahs run like Usain Bolt
Dogs run like Lightning Bolt

And by the way
In answer to Mum's poem
Well trained dogs are allowed
I will grow up soon and have my way

Cats chase mice
Dogs chase cats
Mice like cheese
And hunt them down

# Good Friday

Good Friday

## COLOURS

I love pink.
I love blue.
I love green.
Let me think
Whether I can add orange.

I love yellow.
I love indigo.
I love red.
And colours of the rainbow.
What other colours do you know?

I love black.
I love white.
I love brown.
But don't expect me,
To wear a brown gown.

# Good Friday

# CHAPTER ONE

## GOOD FRIDAY

A very good and the most Holy man this world has ever seen once walked upon the earth. His name, is Jesus. Some call him Christ but I believe His proper title is not Mr Jesus but Jesus the Son of the Most High God or Jesus the Christ. Others call Him Lord Jesus or King Jesus.

### One of His disciples

In those days, I was one of His followers and we were called His Disciples. Jesus loved praying to God and helping people. He said He was here to do His Father's work. A lot of people received miracles from Him. Blind people started seeing

6

again; lepers had new skin; lame people could walk and dead people would wake up. Jesus was so wonderful that a massive crowd of people followed Him everywhere He went. I witnessed this with my very own eyes.

## Jesus had jealous enemies

However not all people liked Jesus. Some pompous religious people, some politicians and those who liked cheating and deceiving innocent people did not like Him. They did not like how His teachings were making people better, happier, and wiser. They even hated Him for healing the sick and had plotted to place Him under arrest, but He always escaped.

# Good Friday

## Service through humility

Jesus knew that His Father had allowed Him to be disliked. So much so that, He knew all about their plots. On the night before His betrayal, Jesus decided to wash the feet of all His Disciples. He was pleased with them because they had served Him well. Besides, Jesus still had lessons for them. This was done to teach them how leaders must be humble and willing to serve and share. He also taught them how to remember Him by breaking and sharing a loaf of bread and drinking wine. Which He called His body and blood.

# CHAPTER TWO

## The plot thickens

So, on Good Friday, Jesus went to pray in the beautiful garden of Gethsemane. When we arrived, Jesus said that I was supposed to be on the look out to warn Him if the guards were coming. And I fell asleep. To cut a long story short however, Jesus has asked us all to watch and pray so that we do not fall into temptation. Anyway, Jesus woke me up in the night because I fell asleep when I was supposed to be keeping watch.

## The betrayal

I was so tired, I disappointed him twice. So, He just continued praying by Himself in a secret place because only He knew exactly what was going to happen. Some of His heart wrenching words were *"Father, if it is Your will, take this cup away from me"*.

9

# Good Friday

However, He had also said, '*not my will but Thine*'. That is very shocking and painful when I think about it. Why would God allow wicked people to kill His only Son whom He called "*my beloved Son, in whom I am well pleased*". I am telling you; Jesus was sweating blood!

Soon after He had finished praying, He returned to join us. He scolded us for not being good friends because I kept falling asleep. The guards came and incredibly, our Friend, His disciple, Judas betrayed Him. Apparently, he had been paid 30 coins of silver by those plotting to kill Jesus. He had agreed with the soldiers that the one he kissed would be Jesus. This enabled them to identify and arrest Jesus. I was shocked and greatly angry. I chopped off the ear of one of the soldiers

# Good Friday

with my sword. Even there, Jesus asked me to calm down and returned the man's ear as if nothing had happened.

It was so scary. How could they destroy an innocent man who did only good things? I thought that I was following the greatest man on earth, but He would not even call down angels or fire from heaven to destroy His enemies. All Jesus wanted was to save the world by dying on a cross.

11

# CHAPTER THREE

**Cursed is anyone who hangs upon a tree**

They were determined to hang him upon the cross. Why would they do that to someone who

# Good Friday

was always being good and healing or feeding or teaching other people?  It was unbelievable that He had to hang upon a tree with bad thieves and murderers.  Only wicked people were hung upon a cross.

It is only now that I am learning that Jesus was made a curse because he bore all our suffering, our curse, infirmities, sin, weaknesses and nailed them upon a cross.  He exchanged that with a blessing for us.  So that we would not be miserable.

When His Mum came to see Him hanging on a wooden cross, she was crying.  Jesus asked for water because He was thirsty.  The wicked soldiers gave Him sponge wet with gall, which was very bitter, and vinegar to quench His thirst. It was disgusting behaviour and a very sad time for His family and disciples to witness.  He did not deserve any punishment.  Why did the crowd have Him crucified?

But Jesus was the powerful Son of God, so by midday, the whole world was in darkness and the sun disappeared.

# Good Friday

Goodness gracious! Then, Jesus said, *"Eli Eli lama sabachthani?"* *"It is finished"*. And then sadly, He died.

And the earth trembled and shook and the church veil tore into two halves. It was very powerful and scary. I thought God was about to come and punish those who had killed Jesus. By this time, Judas had felt so guilty about his actions, that he took his own life. Which was not what Jesus would have wished for him. He could have said he was sorry or beg for forgiveness instead.

Good Friday

# CHAPTER FOUR

## Why I celebrate Easter

Jesus was taken off the cross because a kind Philanthropist called Joseph of Aramathea, wanted to give Him a decent burial. So, he got Jesus laid in a tomb.

But on the third day, Jesus arose from the dead. An angel rolled the stone away from the tomb entrance. Two men in shining garments appeared to Mary in the morning when she was weeping because she could not find Jesus' body in the tomb. They asked her, *"why seek ye the living among the dead"*? At that time, the disciples remembered that Jesus had said He would resurrect on the third day.

15

# Good Friday

## **Jesus proves His resurrection**

Then rumours about his resurrection spread like wildfire. Afterwards there were reported sightings. Eventually, Jesus visited his disciples. At first, they were afraid because they thought

16

# Good Friday

they had seen a ghost. However, Jesus allowed doubting Thomas to touch Him. He then took supper with them. Even though Jesus knew that Simon had denied Him 3 times, Jesus chose Simon Peter to lead the church as we know it today. He left His followers in his care asking him to *"feed my sheep"*. He commanded His Disciples to go into *'all the world'* and preach the gospel to every creature. He promised that signs and wonders would follow His believers. And that my Friends, marked the beginning of the early church.

# Good Friday

♪♪≈≈≈≈≈≈≈≈≈≈≈♪♪

The journey continues because Jesus is still alive.

Come!

Let's go treasure hunting in the next story!

It is because of Easter that Christians thrive.

We shall find Easter eggs.

But what is more important is the gift of all His treasures

We were sad when He was sold and punished.

Crucified.

Buried in a tomb.

Untold pain and suffering for our sake.

Truly we are worth more than Easter eggs.

You and I are forgiven.

Rejoice for He is alive.

And in perfect condition.

It is always a Happy Easter.

We are no longer bereft.

If you have read the Bible.

Tell me, how good is your memory?

Because it is your turn to tell me what happens next.

♪♪≈≈≈≈≈≈≈≈≈≈≈♪♪

Good Friday

# PIRATE TOMMY

## PART II OF TOBY'S KS1 & KS2
## TRILOGY

# CHAPTER FOUR

# I LIKE MR BEAN

I like Mr Bean.
Because he is very funny
He makes me laugh.
He's been to many places
Because I've seen Mr Bean on holiday

His passport belongs to Rowan Atkinson
That is his real name
So he will not be arrested
But he reminds me of bright colours
By the silly clever things he does

I cough with laughter.
Each time I hear his strange chatter
And when he tries to look tough
Or surprised I chuckle
And laugh so hard you'd thing I was tickled

# Good Friday

# Good Friday

# Good Friday

## ABOUT THE AUTHOR

The Author uses Sharon Rose as her pseudonym. Good Friday was created as part of a trilogy and it is followed by Pirate Tommy and Prince Save. All of which were written in London in 2009.

Her works are underpinned by her Christian belief and do not refrain from quoting the Bible. Normally referenced as a yardstick for societal values and morals; or a source of joy, peace, liberty, inspiration, hope, information, knowledge and even entertainment.

Good Friday was first printed with Toby as Author and stick characters drawn by him. This project was created to immortalise his schoolwork from KS1 & KS2.

The Author now lives in Walsall with Toby. Having been on numerous 'adventures' in London, Uganda and The Gambia. Which has now inspired material for books for all age groups.

The Author has a solid legal background training, adjudicating, supporting in Legal Secretarial capacity, proofreading, research and in a paralegal roles. Since returning to the UK in 2019, she has worked in factories, warehouses, a housing association and a mental health clinic. At one point, she was enrolled on an LLM postgraduate degree at the BPP and intends to develop her career.

# Good Friday

Printed in Great Britain
by Amazon

64404194R00020